the party One of

A Souvenir of the Trans-Continental Excursion of Railroad Agents

1870

the party One of

A Souvenir of the Trans-Continental Excursion of Railroad Agents
1870

ISBN/EAN: 9783744727181

Printed in Europe, USA, Canada, Australia, Japan

Cover: Foto ©Andreas Hilbeck / pixelio.de

More available books at **www.hansebooks.com**

CONTENTS.

INTRODUCTION.

THE excursion of September, 1870, of railroad officials over the Pacific Railways, was so perfect and so pleasurable to its participants, that, before the breaking up of the party at Omaha, many of them requested the author to compile and write a brief history of that wonderful trip.

The writer pretends to no peculiar skill as a chronicler of events. He hopes, in these few pages, only to bring to mind and preserve some of the pleasurable incidents, and a general outline of what was to the participants the brightest and most enjoyable tour of their lives.

The route, which the party traversed, has in guide books and by correspondents been described, both generally and in detail. There will be, then, no attempt in the within to any thing more than a mere glancing description of the places and scenes along the route, as necessarily connected with the history of the excursion.

In preparing these pages the writer acknowledges his indebtedness to the reports of newspaper correspondents for many connected facts as regards time and place in relation to the excursion.

INITIATION OF EXCURSION.

The following invitations were issued by the Union and Central Pacific Railroad Companies to the general passenger, ticket and freight agents of the railroads of the United States and Canadas:

CENTRAL AND UNION PACIFIC R. R. LINE.

GENERAL PASSENGER OFFICE, U. P. R. R.,
OMAHA, Nebraska, *August 15th*, 1870.

DEAR SIR:

The general officers of the Central and Union Pacific Railroads unite in extending to you a most cordial invitation to join in a special excursion of the general passenger, ticket and freight agents of the railroads of the United States and Canadas.

A special train of palace sleepers will leave Omaha fifteen days previous to the sitting of the general ticket agents' convention at Milwaukee; and return in time to accommodate those wishing to attend that meeting.

The train will pass, *en route*, Great Salt Lake City, the cañons of the Rocky Mountains, the passes of the Sierras, and other points of interest by daylight.

Please intimate to the general passenger office of the U. P. R. R. at Omaha, by September 1st, your acceptance of this joint invitation, that suitable arrangements may be made. You will be notified of the day and hour of departure from Omaha, as soon as the date of the general ticket agents' convention is definitely fixed.

We trust you will find it convenient to join the excursion, and unite pleasure and rest with business, while studying the new relations existing between the great states and territories west of the Missouri river, and the older states of the South and East; and more especially the questions and necessities arising from the new routes opened up by the Pacific Railway, in connection with the several steamship lines established between San Francisco and the Transpacific ports of India, China, Japan, Australia and the Sandwich Islands; and the ports of the North and South Pacific.

A correct knowledge of all the important facts connected with these new developments can only be obtained by personal investigation. Every railway on the continent is intimately interested. Union and co-operation is required to utilize the advantages arising from the position of our country in relation to the carrying trade between the continents on either side.

Very respectfully,

T. H. GOODMAN, G. P. A. C. P. R. R.

FRANCIS COLTON, G. P. A. U. P. R. R.

C. W. SMITH, G. F. A. C. P. R. R. *and* *President General Freight Agents' Association.*

WM. MARTIN, G. F. A. U. P. R. R

I heartily indorse and recommend the above invitation.

A. A. BARNES,
President General Ticket Agents' Convention.

NOTE.—The wives of the invited officers are included in the above invitation.

Sixteen days after the issue of the foregoing invitation, the time of the general ticket agents' convention at Chicago being fixed, the following notification was sent forth:

UNION AND CENTRAL PACIFIC RAILROAD LINE.

GENERAL PASSENGER DEPARTMENT, UNION PACIFIC RAILROAD,
OMAHA, Nebraska, *August 31st*, 1870.

DEAR SIR:

Respectfully referring to the invitation from this line of August 15th, 1870, asking you to join in an excursion to the Pacific, you are hereby notified that a SPECIAL TRAIN, for the conveyance of those invited, will leave Omaha, September 13th, arriving in San Francisco, Sunday, 18th, or Monday, 19th, according to stops *en route* as the party may wish to make. Returning, leave San Francisco, Friday evening, 23d, arriving in Omaha 27th, and Chicago 28th.

If you should wish to remain in San Francisco a longer time than that indicated above, you can come earlier than the regular day of starting.

Jos. Young, Esq., General Superintendent of the Utah Central Railroad, unites in the invitation, and will take the special train over his road to Salt Lake City and return.

Very respectfully Yours,

T. H. GOODMAN,
G. P. A. C. P. R. R.

FRANS. COLTON,
G. P. A. U. P. R. R.

Immediately on the issue of the foregoing notification, the following generous invitations from roads in immediate connection with the Union and Central Pacific, were sent to all who had been invited by the latter:

Circular No. 22.

Chicago, Rock Island and Pacific Railroad,
Chicago, *September 1st*, 1870.

Dear Sir:

This road, in connection with the Union and Central Pacific Railroads, extends to the general freight, ticket and passenger agents of your road a cordial invitation to join in the excursion to the Pacific coast, leaving Chicago on Monday, September 12th, and arriving at San Francisco, Sunday, September 18th, or Monday, September 19th. Returning, the special train will leave San Francisco Friday evening, 23d, arriving at Chicago in time for the general ticket agents' convention on the 28th.

The ladies of the officers mentioned above are included in this invitation.

Respectfully,

E. St. JOHN,
General Ticket Agent.

LEWIS VIELE,
General Freight Agent.

Approved,
HUGH RIDDLE,
General Superintendent.

Chicago, Burlington and Quincy Railroad Company,
Chicago, *September* 5, 1870.

Dear Sir:

Presuming that you will accept the invitation of the Union and Central Pacific Railroads for their excursion from Omaha to San Francisco, it gives us pleasure to extend the courtesy of the Chicago, Burlington and Missouri River Railroad line from Chicago to Omaha and return, for yourself and lady.

Our train, with Pullman's palace cars will leave Chicago, Monday, 12th inst., at 10:45 A. M., and connect with special train from Omaha on the 13th.

Hoping to have the pleasure of your company,

We are, very respectfully,

SAM'L POWELL,
General Ticket Agent.

E. R. WADSWORTH,
General Freight Agent.

A similar generous invitation was issued from the office of the Chicago and North-western Railway, signed by H. P. Stanwood, G. T. A., and other officers of the road.

CHICAGO TO OMAHA.

By the 12th of September there had gathered at Chicago a majority of the party destined for the Pacific. On that morning, bright and beautiful, extra palace cars were attached for the accommodation of the excursionists, on each of the three railways leading to Council Bluffs.

Some chose one route and some another, more from local curiosity and companionship than from partiality to either route. The party was about equally divided. The writer went by the Chicago and Rock Island road, and was a recipient, with twenty other favored ones, of the kind attentions and multiplied favors of Mr. E. St. John, the gentlemanly general ticket agent of that road. It was a day of unalloyed pleasure.

How could it be otherwise? Passing through the two great agricultural states, Illinois and Iowa, in a regal car, perfect in all its appointments, surrounded by a genial, sensible company, and a perfect autumn day, and you have all the conditions possible for enjoyment. And we did enjoy it, thanks to the road and the gentleman who acted as our host. We shall never forget him, and his amiable and intelligent wife.

Equally pleased and elegantly cared for were those of our number who took the other routes. Mrs. Evarts, in the Chicago Journal, thus speaks of their ride over the North-western: "In the first place, a brand-new car. No second-hand upholstery—no dingy hangings and battered wood-work for us. The wheeled palace we occupied was fresh from the shops. We were the sharers of its virgin trip. H. P. Stanwood, the courteous ticket agent of the North-western, lost no opportunity of making us feel at home and comfortable. The day sped delightfully away in chatting, reading, or looking out upon the beautiful country, as it flashed by in endless panorama of hill, forest and meadow."

A like report did we hear from those who took the Burlington and Quincy route, under the charge of Mr. Samuel Powell, general ticket agent. All spoke in the highest terms of attentions shown them, and the comfort and pleasure experienced on that road.

ARRIVAL AT OMAHA.

At ten o'clock on the morning of the 13th, we reached the banks of the Missouri at Council Bluffs. As we stepped from our palace home, on the landing, we heard the whistles of the trains which bore our fellow excursionists from Chicago, and saw them with us, carpet bags in hand, hastening for the same ferry-boat to cross the river into Omaha. We thought to ourselves, well, railroading is at least approaching perfection, when three trains coursing over five hundred miles, often separated in their routes an hundred miles or more, traversing a widely different region of country, and yet reaching a given point within ten minutes of each other. There are not, probably, in this country three better equipped and worked railroads than the Chicago and Rock Island, the Chicago and North-western, and the Chicago, Burlington and Quincy.

Crossing the river, we were met at the landing by a committee of the Common Council of the city. Carriages were furnished us, many of them private. Here we spent two hours riding through the streets of this wonderful town — a town of but a few brief years, yet now with all the appointments of an old city — substantial buildings, fine blocks of stores, street railroads, elegant hotels, etc. We rode to the court-house hill, where we enjoyed a fine view of the country. Council Bluffs lying at the foot of the hills from which the town takes its name, the winding Missouri for miles around us, the swarming town and the busy levee, met the vision.

At twelve o'clock we were driven to the Wyoming House, where dinner was prepared for us. While the party were partaking of this ample repast, G. W. Frost, Esq., who had acted in the capacity of purchasing agent for the Union Pacific road, and by whose persevering efforts the road was furnished with early supplies, in a short and appropriate speech introduced the councilmen to the excursionists. Mr. E. A. Allen, president of the city council, followed. They both extended the cordial greeting of the city to us all, regretting that our stay was to be so short and our opportunities for seeing so limited. Some of the party expressing the wish to make some acknowledgment for this unexpected reception, Mr. Allen replied: "Gentlemen, the train leaves at 12.20; we will do the talking; we expect you to do the eating."

It would be difficult to exaggerate the courtesy, the heartiness of our reception in the city of Omaha. It was as gratifying as unexpected. Long flourish Omaha and her generous citizens.

The Union Pacific Railroad Company, to whom, in connection with the Central Pacific, we were indebted for the grand excursion upon which we were about to enter, have their principal offices at Omaha, the eastern terminus of their road. Its officers and offices are as follows:

OFFICES AND OFFICERS OF U. P. R. R.

OLIVER AMES, President, Boston, Mass.
JOHN DUFF, Vice-President, " "
J. M. S. WILLIAMS, Treas., " "
E. H. ROLLINS, Secretary, " "
C. G. HAMMOND, General Superintendent, Omaha, Neb.
C. W. MEAD, Assistant Gen'l Superintendent, " "
J. R. NICHOLS, Assistant Superintendent, " "
S. H. H. CLARK, Supt. Platte Division, " "
C. H, CHAPPEL, Supt. Lodge Pole Division, Cheyenne, W. T.
L. FILLMORE, Supt. Laramie & Utah Divs., Laramie, W. T.
T. E. SICKLES, Chief Engineer.
F. COLTON, General Passenger Agent, Omaha, Neb.
B. R. KEIM, Assistant General Passage Agent, "
WM. MARTIN, General Freight Agent, Omaha, Neb.
H. BROWNSON, Assistant General Freight Agent.
A. S. DOWNS, Local Treasurer.
JOS. W. GANNETT, Auditor.
I. H. CONGDON, Superintendent Motive Power.
GEO. E. STEVENS, Master Car Builder.
D. MARTIN, Supt. Bridge Building and Water Departments.
T. W. COOKE, General Agent, Ogden.
J. J. DICKEY, Supt. Telegraph, Omaha, Neb.
O. F. DAVIS, Land Commissioner.

PRINCIPAL OFFICES: Railroad Building, Omaha, Nebraska. Sear's Building, Boston, Mass.

The Union Pacific road comprises the Platte, Lodge Pole, Laramie, and Utah Divisions.

THE START.

After leaving our hospitable friends, we were driven to the train, which was to convey us to Ogden, Utah Territory, the terminus of the Union Pacific. Even to railroad men that train was a pleasant novelty. It was

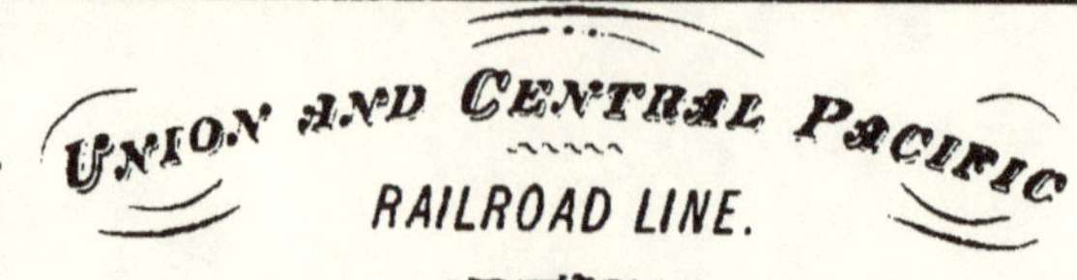

UNION AND CENTRAL PACIFIC

RAILROAD LINE.

EXCURSION

OF THE

General Passenger, Ticket and Freight Agents

OF THE

UNITED STATES AND CANADAS.

COMPLIMENTARY

Omaha to San Francisco and Return.

For Mr.

R. R.

T. H. GOODMAN,
G. P. A. C. P. R. R.

FRANS. COLTON,
G. P. A. U. P. R. R.

Good until Sept. 15, '70, Westward. | *Good until Oct.* [illegible]*, '70, Eastward.*

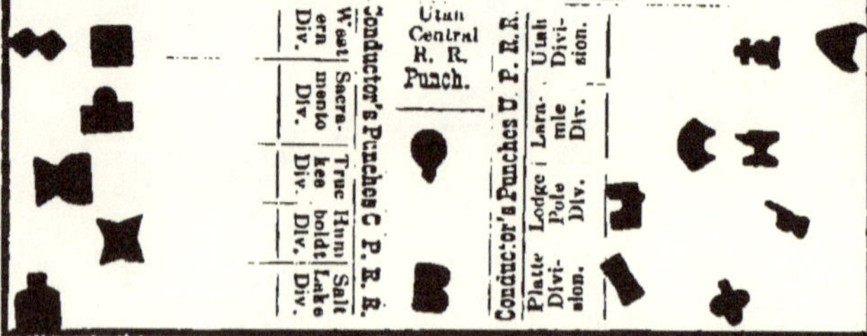

truly, as Mr. Colton, the passenger agent of the road, designated it, "the fancy train." It consisted of five Pullman palace drawing-room and sleeping cars, one smoking car and one baggage car. Two of the coaches were new, with stationary organs, couches and easy chairs—and all of them palaces of luxury and comfort.

In these splendid residences, on wheels, we were soon comfortably housed. Before moving off on the long road before us, a ticket was handed to each one of the party. It was elegantly gotten up, and inclosed in book covers, with appropriate superscriptions on its lids. (See fac simile of ticket on opposite page.)

The following list of the party was consummated at San Francisco, most of whom were on the train at Omaha. A few joined us at Denver, Salt Lake City and Ogden.

LIST OF EXCURSIONISTS.

Joseph W. Allen, General Ticket Agent W. J. and C. M. and M. Railroads, Camden, New Jersey.

W. R. Allen, General Ticket Agent Iron Mountain Railroad, St. Louis, Missouri.

Chas. H. Abbott, General Freight and Ticket Agent Cincinnati & Muskingum Valley R. R., Zanesville, Ohio.

James F. Aglar, General Manager Far West Fast Freight Line, St. Louis.

Mrs. Jas. F. Aglar.

John N. Bofinger, President St. Louis and New Orleans Packet Co., St. Louis, Mo.

Mrs. John N. Bofinger.

Wm. H. Bryant, General Ticket Agent Rutland and Burlington and Vermont Valley Railroad, Rutland, Vermont.

E. B. Byington, General Ticket Agent Merchants' Southern Packet Line, St. Louis.

Geo. A. Brown, General Ticket Agent Cheshire Railroad, Keene, N. H.

H. P. Baldwin, General Passenger Agent Allentown Line, New York.

Mrs. H. P. Baldwin.

Mrs. O. L. Baldwin.

Mrs. M. E. Barnes, La Porte, Indiana.

E. A. Brown, General Ticket Agent Boston, Clinton and Fitchburg Railroad, Fitchburg, Mass.

Mrs. E. A. Brown.

O. E. Britt, General Freight Agent Milwaukee and St. Paul R. R., Milwaukee, Wisconsin.

Mrs. O. E. Britt, Milwaukee, Wisconsin.

Miss Kate E. Britt, Milwaukee, Wisconsin.

James C. Boyden, General Freight and Ticket Agent Saint Paul and Sioux City Railroad, St. Paul, Minnesota.

W. W. Botkin, Correspondent *Chicago Times*.

F. Chandler, General Ticket Agent St. Louis, Vandalia, Terre Haute and Indianapolis Railroad, St. Louis.

Miss M. L. Chandler, Chicago.

Mrs. Henry Crocker, Memphis, Tennessee.

E. J. Cartledge, St. Louis and St. Joseph Railroad General Freight and Ticket Agent, Saint Joseph, Missouri.

Mrs. E. J. Cartledge.

D. O. Calder, General Freight and Ticket Agent Utah Central Railroad, Salt Lake City.

Ann H. Calder, Salt Lake City.

W. W. Chandler, Agent Star Union Line, Chicago, Illinois.

Mrs. W. W. Chandler.

Lewis Carvell, General Superintendent Government Railways in New Brunswick, St. John, New Brunswick.

George Q. Cannon, Editor Deseret *Evening News*, Salt Lake City, Utah.

Mrs. George Q. Cannon and child.

George W. Cobb, Superintendent Mineral Point Railroad, Mineral Point, Wisconsin.

Mrs. George W. Cobb.

H. H. Courtright, General Freight Agent Hannibal and Saint Joseph Railroad, Hannibal, Missouri.

Mrs. H. H. Courtright.

John T. Caine, Managing Editor Salt Lake *Herald*, Salt Lake City, Utah.

Mrs. John T. Caine, Salt Lake City, Utah.

Geo. A. Dadmun, General Ticket Agent Philadelphia, Wilmington & Baltimore R. R., Philadelphia.

Mrs. George A. Dadmun.

A. C. Davis, General Ticket Agent Belvidere, Delaware and Flemington Railroad, Lambertville, N. J.

Miss M. L. Everts, Correspondent Chicago *Evening Journal*, Chicago.

J. G. Everest, South-east Passenger Agent C. & N. W. Railway.

Miss Mary Fisher, Sister of the Superintendent Denver Pacific Railroad, Denver. Colorado.

A. H. Fracker, Master of Transportation of the North Pennsylvania Railroad, Philadelphia.

Mrs. A. H. Fracker.

Wm. S. Freeman, Assistant General Freight Agent Camden & Amboy Railroad, Philadelphia.

Chas. E. Follett, General Passenger and Ticket Agent Ohio and Mississippi Railroad, St. Louis, Missouri.

Mrs. Chas. E. Follett.

John B. Fleming, St. Louis *Times*, St. Louis.

A. A. Folsom, Superintendent Boston and Providence R. R., Boston, Mass.

Mrs. A. A. Folsom.

A. B. Garrison, St. Louis and Pacific Express Freight Company General Freight Agent, St. Louis, Missouri.

Jno. H. Grant, President Eng. Atlantic and West Point Railroad, Atlanta, Georgia.

J. W. Gore, General Ticket Agent Camden and Amboy Railroad, Philadelphia, Pennsylvania.

Mrs. J. W. Gore.

P. B. Groat, General Ticket Agent Hannibal and St. Joseph Railroad, Hannibal, Missouri.

L. P. Grant, Superintendent A. and W. P. Railroad, Atlanta, Georgia.

Charles S. Gauntt, Master Trans. Camden and Amboy Railroad, Burlington, New Jersey.

C. G. Hancock, General Ticket Agent Philadelphia and Rdg. Company, Philadelphia, Pennsylvania.

Amos T. Hall, Treasurer Chicago, Burlington and Quincy Railroad, Chicago.

Mrs. Amos T. Hall and two sons.

A. B. Hull, General Freight Agent Danbury and Norwalk Railroad, Danbury, Connecticut.

Mrs. A. B. Hull.

John Hinton, General Freight Agent L. & B. R. R., Kingston, Pennsylvania.

Mrs. John Hinton.

W. F. Holwill, General Ticket Agent Delaware, Lackawanna and Western Railroad, New York.

Starr S. Jones, Bt. Agent Morgan Line and Mobile and Ohio Railroad, Galveston, Texas.

E. St. John, General Ticket Agent Chicago, Rock Island and Pacific Railroad, Chicago, Illinois.

Mrs. E. St. John.

Thos. L. Kimball, General Western Passenger Agent Pennsylvania Central Railroad, Chicago.

Beverley R. Keim, Assistant General Passenger Agent Union Pacific Railroad, Omaha.

Mrs. Beverly R. Keim.

Frank A. Mackenzie, Passenger Agent General Transatlantic Company, New York city.

F. R. Myers, General Passenger and Ticket Agent Pittsburgh, Fort Wayne and Chicago Railway, Chicago, Illinois.

Mrs. F. R. Myers.

John McMillan, European & N. A. Ry., St. John, New Brunswick.

A. J. Mead, General Freight and Ticket Agent, Winona and St. Peter Railroad, Winona, Minnesota.

Miss M. E. Mead, with the above, Genesee, Illinois.

M. Mills, General Freight Agent West Jersey Railroad, Camden, N. J.

D. A. McKinlay, General Ticket Agent Dubuque South-western Railroad, Dubuque, Iowa.

Mrs. D. A. McKinlay.

Mrs. Mayall, St. Paul, Minnesota.

Loyal S. Nye, President Nye Forwarding Company, Denver, Colorado.

Mrs. L. S. Nye.

George Olds, General Ticket Agent Kansas City, St. Joseph & C. B. R. R., St. Joseph, Missouri.

Mrs. George Olds.

C. P. Oakley, General Ticket and Freight Agent Mississippi and Tennessee Railroad, Memphis, Tennessee.

Mrs. C. P. Oakley.

Master Walter D. Oakley, Memphis, Tennessee.

Samuel Powell, General Ticket Agent Chicago, Burlington and Quincy Railroad, Chicago, Illinois.

Mrs. Samuel Powell.

John U. Parsons, General Ticket Agent Toledo, Wabash and Western Railroad, Toledo, Ohio.

Mrs. John U. Parsons.

Fred. W. Rankin, Secretary of the New Jersey Railroad and Transportation Company, New York city.

Mrs. Fred. W. Rankin.

J. Roberts, of General Freight Department Belvidere, Delaware and Flemington Railroad, Lambertville, New Jersey.

Wm. Rhodes, General Freight and Ticket Agent North-western Union Packet Company, St. Paul, Minnesota.

Mrs. Wm. Rhodes.

Justus E. Ralph, General Ticket Agent New Jersey Southern Railroad, Red Bank, New Jersey.

Miss Gussie Shewell, St. Louis, Missouri.

H. P. Stanwood, General Ticket Agent Chicago and North-western Railway, Chicago.

Mrs. H. P. Stanwood.

Jno. Shaw, Traveling Agent Inman Steamship Company, New York.

C. A. Savage, President Quincy, Missouri and Pacific Railroad, Quincy, Illinois.

Mrs. C. A. Savage.

Henry Starring, General Baggage Agent Pittsburg to San Francisco.

L. M. E. Stone, Superintendent P. W. & B. R. R., Providence, Rhode Island.

Mrs. L. M. E. Stone.

E. S. Tracy, General Freight Agent Chicago, Cincinnati and Louisville Railroad, La Porte, Indiana.

Morris E. Ward, correspondent, Denver, Colorado.

Miss K. Wheedon, St. Louis, Missouri.

George S. Wright, General Ticket Agent Worcester and Nashua Railroad, Worcester, Massachusetts.

J. M. Williams, General Freight Agent Worcester and Nashua Railroad, Worcester, Massachusetts.

Thos. A. Weed, Scottsville, New York.

Wm. H. Weed, General Ticket Agent New York and Oswego Midland Railroad, Oswego, New York.

E. N. Winslow, Superintendent and Treasurer Cape Cod Railroad, Hyams, Massachusetts.

Mrs. E. N. Winslow.

Having been assigned our respective places in "the fancy train," on we moved, and the continental trip was fully initiated.

As we slowly ascended the bluffs of the Missouri, and began to look out on the vast prairie that sweeps up to its shore, we were silent, thoughtful, meditative. Soon from the windows of our palace homes there stretched before us and around us, an ocean of land — nothing but the curve of the earth itself obstructed the vision — not a hill, shrub or tree met the eye. There was almost an ominous stillness over that vast plain; only the low rumbling of our train, as it sped, arrow-like, over its bosom, broke the silence. At times, in a kind of soliloquy, you would hear the exclamation, "How grand!" "How beautiful!"

PLATTE RIVER.

Soon we reach a "station" like a stopping place mid-ocean — an acre-island in the Atlantic. We take in fuel and water, and speed on. Then it is announced that the far-famed Platte river is in view on our left; all rush to the windows to get a sight of a stream of which we had heard and read so much. What a relief to the eye was its placid waters, and the few cotton woods that skirted its banks. Then, as we ran along its shore for hundreds of miles, there came to our minds the scenes that had been enacted so recently on its banks — the emigrant trains that had sunk in its treacherous fords — the Indian butcheries by its side — the vast herds of buffaloes and horses which had roamed from its mysterious sources, in the fastnesses of the Rocky Mountains, to where it mingled its waters with those of the turbid Missouri. We never got wearied in those hundreds of miles of looking at its waters, and following its track by the low shrubbery on its banks.

Night came upon us, shutting us up to ourselves. We had been thrown together, mostly strangers to each other, hailing from nearly every state of the Union, and the Canadas. The usual stiffness and unsociableness characterizing such circumstances soon began to give way. We were to be the companions of weeks, and sought early to know and fellowship each other. Before the retirement that first evening, much had been done to make us one family, with the usual cousins, uncles and aunts. We closed our eyes in sleep, on that first night, with the comfortable feeling, that we had a propitious beginning and a joyful prospect before us.

The morning broke upon us beautiful and inspiring. All had been refreshed by sleep undisturbed. So smooth was the iron track, and so comfortable our couches, that we scarcely realized our absence from our accustomed places of sleep.

Still all around us were the trackless plains. Occasionally we discovered in the distance highlands or bluffs. Now, too, we began to see a few wild animals, for which we had been straining our eyes ever since leaving Omaha. Now and then a few antelopes could be seen, literally "dusting" to clear the terrible locomotive and the less terrible "shooting-irons" of the party. Scarcely one was passed that did not receive the compliment of a dozen or more pistol shots. At first this shooting at the poor innocents was considered by the ladies and the older gentlemen of the party as cruelty in the extreme. But all soon learned to spend no sympathy on the antelope, as from Omaha to San Francisco and back, not one was hit, or seemingly disturbed by the bullets hurled at them. We learned this fact, that whatever else railroad men *could* do, they could not shoot. And we here offer this admonition to them, never to become involved in an affair of honor, where shooting may be the sequel.

During the day we passed what was called "Prairie Dog City." Here, for miles beside the track, we saw the holes of these "dogs." On the approach of the train they would come out and sit at the mouth of their holes, and look with a sort of inquiring wonder at the passing train. One of our number, a near-sighted gentleman, exhibited a great anxiety to see these "dogs," but was unable. We assured him that the failure was not afflictive, as he had only to imagine a magnified gutter rat, of the dirtiest hue, and he had the "prairie dog." We were told that the Indians used to subsist almost entirely on these animals when grasshoppers became scarce. Individually we should prefer the grasshoppers for a "steady diet."

CHEYENNE.

After passing many places of interest, and scenery attractive and beautiful, we reach Cheyenne, the capital of Wyoming territory, and the largest town out of Omaha on the Union Pacific Railroad, five hundred and sixteen miles from the Missouri river. Here we found a city with its bustle and business, and here we had a capital dinner, and availed ourselves of the generous privilege tendered us by the Western Union and Atlantic and Pacific Telegraph Companies of sending communications free to our friends. In this town are extensive shops of the railroad company; a round-house and machine and repair shops, substantial buildings of stone.

DENVER.

Here, too, is the junction of the Denver Pacific road with the Union Pacific. At the request of the officers of the former our train was transferred to their road, and the party taken to Denver, the capital of Colorado, where we arrived at 4 P. M. on Wednesday.

The country through which we passed on our excursion into Colorado was a little more diversified, but mostly a vast plain, inhabited by the antelope, wolf, and prairie dog. Some of the way our road ran along in sight of the south fork of the Platte river, its course marked by the only shrubbery or green vegetation in the whole sweep of the eye. This fork of the Platte has its sources in the eastern, as the north fork has its in the western, slope of the Rocky Mountains. Each of them pursues a generaly north-east course for about three hundred miles, and then turns to the eastward, uniting some three hundred miles eastward of the mountains, where the plains melt into the prairies. Between these two rivers and the eastern base of the mountains, there is formed an immense triangle, upon which, in common with our present territories and the states of Nevada and California, no rain falls between April and November, yet from the facilities for irrigation from the Platte and its tributaries, the depth and richness of the soil, it will no doubt, at an early day, be ranked among the finest agricultural portions of our country.

Half way between Cheyenne and Denver is the town of Greeley, named after the far-famed Horace. Here, under the lead of Mr. Meeker, the founder of the colony, a village has sprung up since April last of some five hundred inhabitants. Our party spent an hour in rambling about this mushroom place. The inhabitants seemed a little homesick, and apparently relished our raid among them. Mr. Meeker told us that they were "probably on the best piece of land in the United States." He had had before him the American continent, and this was the spot *above* all other; and so taking leave of Greeley we took the train and moved on toward Denver.

Soon the Rocky Mountains appeared in the distance, some fifty miles away to our right. This, to some of us, was our first sight of mountains. As seen in the misty distance, lying along the horizon, with their irregular peaks or hommocks touching the skies, we could think of nothing but a vast caravan of gigantic dromedaries lying down for the repose of night. As we approached Denver we were within fifteen miles of the foot hills of the mountains. While in that city we caught a view of the noted Pike's Peak, sixty-five miles south of us.

At Denver we partook of a good dinner at the American House — and then "did up the city." As we walked around the place with one of the citizens, he gave us many reminiscenses of the early history of the town, its gambling dens, the desperate encounters of the early miners, the murders, etc. Occasionally he would point to a bridge-post, or an old stub of cotton-wood and tell us that they were favorite hanging places, in the olden times, (*i. e.* eight years ago); we felt a slight uneasiness, and a few chills, but said nothing. Here is now a city of 10,000 inhabitants, well laid out streets, fine blocks of stores, well appointed hotels, and all the stir and activity which so characterize western towns. The country around is open and rolling. A few miles to the west, and the Rocky Mountains raise their towering peaks. Denver can be said to lie at the foot of these mountains. To the east stretches the vast plain, without a break, six hundred miles to the Missouri river.

While in Denver, Col. T. J. Carter, President of the Colorado Central Road, invited the party to take a trip on his road, as far as completed. About twenty accepted the invitation, and went as far as the rails were laid, where they were met by almost the entire population of Golden City, who loudly cheered and welcomed them as being on the train which had first passed over their road.

A few of the party, who remained in Denver, indulged in a dance at the American, which, judging from the price paid for this luxury, was considered a clincher on the old adage — " he who dances must pay the fiddler."

At midnight, we left the capital of Colorado for Cheyenne, having added to our number the genial

L. S. Nye and his amiable wife; also, the companionable and very acceptable Morris E. Ward, Esq., citizens of Denver.

ROCKY MOUNTAINS.

When we awoke on the morning of the 15th, we had ascended the Rocky Mountains. As we stepped out at Sherman, 8,000 feet above the level of the sea, there was a frosty crispness about the air. We gathered our outer garments closely around us, and ran about the place, enjoying hugely the rarefied but inspiriting atmosphere. Here, at this elevation, we had a grand view of the surrounding country: 75 miles to the south, Long's Peak towered above its fellows; 165 miles away is Pike's Peak, both visible to the unaided eye, or at least so we were told, and so read in the guide-book. We are confident that we saw them, for we distinctly saw the man and the book that told us we did.

Soon we were at Laramie, having passed, after leaving Sherman, many places of interest, among them the noted Dale Creek bridge, 650 feet long and 126 feet high. At Laramie we partook of a most excellent breakfast, at as well kept a hotel as can be found on the line of any eastern road. Here we should have been glad to have spent a week. It was the most liveable place we had met since leaving the Missouri.

After a ramble of an hour about this home-like town, the train moved on across the Laramie plains, said to be the finest pasturage ground on the continent. Elk mountain, seen from Laramie, was in sight for hundreds of miles in this passage over the Rocky Mountain range. It was, with its rugged sides and snow-capped summit, a conspicuous landmark.

Among us there were some genuine lovers of nature, those who could take in a scene of grandeur and sublimity. In this passage, through the gorges and over the plains of the 500 miles of the Rocky Mountain elevation, all such had a rare treat.

THE INSIDE OF THE TRAIN.

And this leads us to take a view of the inside of the train. We had the usual make up of a country village, the different characters of a well-ordered community; so that we were not dependent for pleasure and enjoyment alone on the moving panorama outside of our wheeled home. When night shut in upon us, we had our enjoyments, our calls from car to car, our little circles where we talked over subjects grave and comical. Choirs were extemporized, and better singing we have rarely heard. All the variety of cultivated mind was with us, which made the excursion one continued enjoyable picnic. Not for a day, or even an hour, did time drag heavily upon our hands. There were the shrewd, comical, discriminating and companionable Chandler, Boyden, Powell, St. John, Hinton, Courtright, Aglar, etc. There were the matter-of-fact and genial Hull, Brown, Cobb, Dadman, Davis, Myers, Mead, Folsom, etc. Then there were the grave, dignified and quietly shrewd Savage, Follett, Carvell, Stanwood, Rankin, Stone, Freeman, etc. For a marvel, there was not a single wiseacre aboard.

But the excursion would have been greatly deficient without the presence of the ladies. A more genial, intelligent company of ladies were never brought together on an excursion. They made those palace cars splendid homes, with all the pleasures and refinements of the best fireside.

Let no man make this great continental trip without his wife or lady friend. Some of us, in thoughtlessness or otherwise, left ours at home. It was an oversight — a mistake; and were it not that others of our party had been more thoughtful and wise, much of our pleasure would have been wanting. The journey is too vast, the scenery is too varied, to be enjoyed fully, without such genial influences. And then, too, an intelligent lady is a greater admirer of nature, has a keener discrimination, and can point out more readily than man the sublimities, grandeur and beauties of passing scenes.

And now with such a company of ladies, fertile in expedients to make every hour contribute its pleasure, we had, to round out the whole, Beverley R. Keim, the assistant passenger agent of the Union Pacific, watching over our comfort with unceasing diligence, anticipating our every want, and supplying them before we had imagined them. He ever presented a cheerful, sunny face. Quick in perception, prompt in action, he was a *sine qua non*, which, liberally rendered, means *an indispensable.* In all his efforts for our comfort and pleasure, he was warmly seconded by his amiable wife, who accompanied us in this journey.

While crossing the mountain ranges, through the kindness of the conductors and engineers, many of us enjoyed the privilege of riding on the engine, which, in that region of plains, gorges and cañons, was a rare treat. It was the place to take in the whole scene, in its picturesque beauty and awful grandeur. Never shall we forget the ride upon the engine in the Rocky and Sierra ranges. Now coursing like a bird over table lands—now suddenly dashing through a cañon between lofty ledges of rocks and mountain sides—then suddenly enveloped in the darkness of a tunnel—stunned by the roar of the train, pent up by its narrow sides—such a ride was worth, alone, a trip across the continent. And none of our party enjoyed it more appreciatingly than many of the ladies. So firmly bedded was the track, so powerful and perfect the engines, that our confidence was soon secured and all fear banished, no emotion being elicted but that of awed pleasure.

At Carbon we make a stop. Much interest was manifested by all in examining the coal mines at this point, several of the company descending the shaft and viewing this valuable and indispensable article in its native state. This mine of coal, of valuable quality and inexhaustible in quantity, must be of immense importance to the railroad company and to the inhabitants on its line.

FORT FRED. STEELE.

After passing through some wild and weird scenery, resembling the ruins of a great city or abandoned massive fortifications, the train brought up suddenly at Fort Steele, one of the most important military posts on the Pacific road. The railroad skirts one side, and the North Platte the rear, of this really beautiful spot. Naturally a wild and rough place, it has been rendered attractive by the industry and good taste of the companies stationed here. The party alighted and walked about the grounds, visiting the quarters of the soldiers and calling on the officers.

The colonel in command, a celebrated Indian fighter, showed us through his quarters, filled with the spoils of his contests with the red men. He gave us, in detail, the mode of Indian warfare—

their manner of approach and attack, and the tactics most successful in meeting them.

Upon the walls around us hung the weapons of Indian warfare and torture. The full dress of a chief, a trophy of the gallant colonel, was transferred from the wall to one of our party, a large and powerfully built man. The disguise was almost perfect. Thus equipped, he set forth with a whoop and a ugh, and made the tour of the grounds, to the astonishment and consternation of many of the party, not aware of the disguise. His shrewd wife, however, soon detected the cheat, not by the ears, as of old, in the fable, but by the formidable mustache of her lord. . She promptly proclaimed the imposition, and thus vanished the painful illusion, and the thoughts of rent chignons and lost scalps.

An hour was delightfully spent in this interesting station. Thanks to the colonel for that pleasant time at Fort Steele.

EVENING PLEASURES.

Night comes upon us while gradually descending to the valley of the Salt Lake. The scenes without are shut in by impenetrable darkness, but all is light and cheerful within our rushing train. Here and there, in gathered circles, we hear the ringing laugh, the result of a well-told anecdote or the pertness of a well-put repartee, or the sharp solution of a difficult conundrum. In one corner, comfortably reclining on sofas, is a party of gentlemen in the afternoon of life, talking up railroads generally, and the Pacific roads in particular. In another car all have resolved themselves into a singing-school, and are discoursing agreeable music.

And then, when conversation begins to lag and the singers grow hoarse—the porters about to prepare our sleeping apartments—here comes the "excursion band," under the lead of Mr. Starring. The instruments are of the most simple class—the violin, fife, flute, tambourine and bones—instruments hastily gathered at Omaha, form the equipment of this unique band. *Thorough rehearsals were had during the day in the baggage car.* Passing through each car, with measured tread, and discoursing timely music, each night, this never-to-be-forgotten band put us all in the best of humor for our night's repose.

At the break of day the porter arouses us with the welcome information that in half an hour we shall reach our breakfast station, where brook trout will form the staple of the meal. All is astir instantly in the cars. At the station we make a rush, fearing the trout will not "go round;" but our fears are soon quieted by the sight of the long tables laden with these delicious fish in superabundance. On leaving that station, pricking our teeth, we said, "That was not a very bad breakfast—that Green river trout breakfast—not very."

ECHO AND WEBER CAÑONS.

Pushing on westward, we soon enter the famous cañons leading into the valley of Great Salt Lake. Here the scenery was absorbing, grand and sublime. Echo and Weber cañons, gorges cut in the mountains by the Weber river, cannot be described in words; seated in the observation car, the eye alone can measure the sublimity. The river, along which our road lay, flows with a rapid current over a bed of water-worn stones and fallen rocks of all sizes, from pebbles to immense blocks of the adjacent mountain. At some points the precipitous sides of this passage become almost vertical. The mountains rise, we judge, from 1,500 to 2,500 feet above the river, and are separated at the base by different widths, in which the river winds from side to side, frequently impinging against the base of the mountains. Down through this awful gulf our train moved swiftly and smoothly; while we were entranced by the granduer and sublimity of the scene passing like a swiftly unrolling panorama before us.

Besides the absorbing scene around us, our thoughts reverted to the thrilling adventures which had transpired in this now celebrated passage. How here many an emigrant had met in deadly encounter the savages—how here, the Mormons had piled up rocks to roll down upon Johnston's army, should it attempt this passage into their valley. Here we remembered the thrilling incident related by a Utah Indian, characteristic of the nerve and war habits of his race. He was threading this pass at midnight, accompanied by his squaw only, both mounted upon the same horse, and the night so dark that he could neither see the outlines of the mountains, nor the ground at his horse's feet, when he heard a sound so slight as scarcely to be perceptible to an Indian's ear, of an arrow carried in the hand, striking once only with a slight tick against the bow. Stopping, he could hear nothing, but instantly dismounted, his squaw leaning upon the horse that she might by no possibility be seen, and placed his ear to the ground, when he heard the same sound repeated but a few feet distant, and was, therefore, satisfied, that, however imminent the danger, he had not yet been heard or seen, for no Indian would make such a noise at night in approaching his foe; he therefore instantly arose, and took his horse by the bridle close to its mouth to lessen the chances of his moving or whinnying, and one hundred and seventy of his deadly enemies, the Sioux, on a war party, filed past him within almost arm's reach, while he remained unobserved.

Emerging suddenly into the valley of Utah, we are surrounded on every side by the pasturage grounds of the Mormons. At noon on Friday we are at Ogden, the terminus of the Union Pacific and the junction of the Central Pacific and Utah Central roads.

Here the party were received by the officers of the Central Pacific. After an interchange of congratulations and introductions, our train was switched on to the Utah Central, and we were on our way to the "city of the saints."

For a while our course was near the east shore of the famous Salt Lake, which, of course, attracted the attention of all — a lake, 20 by 140 miles, containing seven islands, all of rugged mountains, and its surface 4,200 feet above the level of the sea.

SALT LAKE CITY.

Soon the train rounded its head and was moving into the city of the prophet; all rushed to the windows and the platforms to catch a view of the far-famed place. Equally anxious, apparently, were the inhabitants to see the "fancy train," whose arrival had been announced. The streets were filled — door-yards and fences were covered with children. One irreverent fellow, sitting beside us, involuntarily cried out, "Jerusalem! see the young ones." We nudged him, and suggested that we were the guests of the city, and should utter nothing suggestive of disapprobation; he promised to restrain himself. Carriages were at the depot to convey us to the hotel. President Young being absent from the city, and the next in authority, Joseph Young, being sick, we had no public reception. But while partaking of a most excellent dinner at the Townsend House, a message of welcome was received, and guides furnished to show us all places of interest about the city. Thus guided, the party visited the tabernacle, city hall, museum, theater, etc. We found the city orderly, neat and beautiful. Industry and good taste were exhibited in all that met the eye. For location and surroundings we doubt whether, in beauty and grandeur, it has its equal in the United States. All fully realized the description given by a recent traveler, who, standing a little to the west of the city, says: "Behind us were the great Salt Lake and the greater mountains. On our right was the shining Jordan. Beyond it was a strip of valley, then smooth mountain slopes, blending and intermingling, sea-green at the base and dark slate toward the summits. Before us was the city, with its flashing streams, its low, drab, adobe houses, with trellised verandas; its green gardens and deep shade-trees of locust, aspen, poplar, maple, walnut, elder and cotton wood; its bustling marts of trade and cloistered retreats for the offices of a strange religion.

"Beyond it, for many miles, stretched the green, flowery valley, with its blue lakes shimmering in the sun, and bounded at last by an abrupt wall of mountain. On our left still towered the range, rough and jagged with crevices; its solid base green and gray; its rugged summits white with eternal snow. Side by side, grouped and blended, were summer and winter, Italy and Switzerland; the dreamy orient and the restless heart of the west."

Such is Salt Lake city and its environs. We would have gladly spent days in this favored place of nature. But after treading its streets, visiting its shops, stores, museums, theater, city hall, and standing upon the dome of its great temple and looking down upon the whole and off upon its mountain walls, and after receiving, on all sides, the courtesies and good cheer of its citizens, at 7 P. M. we were on our way to

OGDEN,

Where we were transferred from the Pullman palace cars of the Union Pacific to the silver palace cars of the Central Pacific railroad. Six of these magnificent coaches, with smoking and baggage cars, were provided for us. In addition, the superintendent's car, laden with refreshments and fruits, the gift of the generous San Franciscans, brought up the rear. A more beautiful train never stood at a depot to receive a more grateful party.

Here, at Ogden, were added to our company several railroad and newspaper officials of Utah, and some few others who missed the train at Omaha. Here, also, Mr. J. C. Furgeson, correspondent of the Alta Californian, joined us, and remained with us until we left the pier at Oakland, on our return. Mr. F. contributed greatly to our entertainment by his affableness and general knowledge of the country through which we passed, and the Pacific coast.

Mr. T. H. Goodman, general passenger agent, and Mr. Chas. W. Smith, general freight agent of the Central Pacific, took us in charge. Mr. Keim, who had been our acceptable host thus far, subsidied into one of the happy party.

The following programme was distributed through the train :

PROGRAMME.

GENERAL PASSENGER TICKET AND FREIGHT AGENTS'

1870. JOINT CALIFORIA EXCURSION. 1870.

Special Train. C. P. R. R. Programme.

FRIDAY,	September	16,	leave	Ogden - - -	8:00 P. M.	
SATURDAY,	"	17,	arrive	Elko - - -	10:00 A. M.	Breakfast.
"	"	"	"	Battle Mountain -	3:00 P. M.	Dinner.
"	"	"	"	Humboldt - -	8:00 "	Supper.
SUNDAY,	"	18,	"	Summit, - - -	7:00 A. M.	Breakfast.
"	"	"	"	Colfax, - - -	2:00 P. M.	Dinner.
"	"	"	"	Sacramento - -	6:30 P. M.	

And arrive at San Francisco Sunday evening or Monday morning.

RETURNING.

FRIDAY, September 23, leave	San Francisco	-	6:45 P. M.
" " " "	Oakland Pier -	- -	7:30 "
SATURDAY, " 24, arrive	Alta - - - - - -	-	for breakfast.
" " " "	Humboldt, - - - - -	-	for dinner.
SUNDAY, " 25, "	Ogden - - - - - - -	-	11:00 A. M.

The gentlemen of the party, while in San Francisco, are respectfully requested to meet, daily, in the "Museum" room of the Mercantile Library Building, on Bush street, between Montgomery and Sansome streets, at 11 A. M., for consultation, and also whereby notice can be given of any possible change of the programme.

The following list comprises the officers and principal offices of the

CENTRAL PACIFIC RAILROAD.

PRINCIPAL OFFICES.

415 California St., San Francisco. 56 and 58 K St., Sacramento.
54 William St., New York City. 303 Broadway, New York City.

LELAND STANFORD - - - President.
C. P. HUNTINGTON - - - - First Vice-President.
CHARLES CROCKER - - - - Second Vice-President.
MARK HOPKINS - - - - - Treasurer.
E. B. CROCKER - - - - - - Attorney and General Agent.
E. H. MILLER, JR. - - - - - Secretary.
W. H. PORTER - - - - - - Auditor.
S. S. MONTAGUE - - - - - Chief Engineer.
B. B. REDDING - - - - - - Land Commissioner.
J. R. WATSON - - - - - - General Supply Agent.
F. L. VANDENBURGH - - - Superintendent Telegraph.
A. N. TOWNE - - - - - - - General Superintendent.
JOHN CORNING - - - - - Ass't General Superintendent.
E. C. FELLOWS - - Sup't Western & Visalia Divisions

F. W. BOWEN - - - - - -	Sup't Sacramento & Oregon Div's.
C. D. MONTAYNE - - - - -	Sup't Truckee Division.
C. E. GILLETT - - - - - -	Sup't Humboldt Division.
JAS. CAMPBELL - - - - - -	Sup't Salt Lake Division.
F. KNOWLAND - - - - - -	General Eastern Agent.
HENRY STARRING - - - -	General Baggage Agent.
CHAS. W. SMITH - - - - -	General Freight Agent.
T. H. GOODMAN - - - - - -	General Passenger Agent.

THE CENTRAL PACIFIC RAILROAD DIVISIONS

COMPRISE:

	Miles.
The SALT LAKE DIVISION, Ogden to Toano - - - - - - - -	182
HUMBOLDT DIVISION, Toano to Winnemucca - - - - - -	237
TRUCKEE DIVISION, Winnemucca to Truckee - - - - - -	204
SACRAMENTO DIVISION, Truckee to Sacramento - - - -	120
WESTERN DIVISION, Sacramento to San Francisco - - - -	138
OREGON DIVISION, Junction to Soto - - - - - - - - - (Now building to the Oregon State Line.)	92
VISALIA DIVISION, Lathrop to Stanislaus River - - - - - - (Now building to Visalia and south.)	12
SAN JOSE BRANCH, Niles to San Jose - - - - - - - - -	18
S. F. AND OAKLAND RAILROAD, San Francisco to Brooklyn	8
S. F. AND ALAMEDA RAILROAD, San Francisco to Hayward's	21
Total now being operated - - - - - - - - - - - -	1,032

And now the train moves on, around the head of Salt Lake, passing, during the night, many places of interest, among them Brigham city, Corrine, Bear river, noted in the reports of early discoverers, and the scenes occurring to the early emigrants. During this night's ride, we passed over much territory worth seeing, which was viewed with deep interest on our return by the light of day.

The morning broke upon us coursing over the great "American desert," an area of about sixty miles square. It was desolate and lonely—the bare beds of alkali or wastes of gray sand alone meet the eye. It is plausibly conjectured that this desert was once the bed of a saline lake, perhaps a portion of the Great Salt Lake itself.

As we looked out upon these shoreless wastes, there came to us forcibly the words of scripture: "The whole land thereof is brimstone and salt and burning, that it is not sown, nor beareth, nor any grass groweth therein."

On this desert, as all along the road from Omaha, we see the low mud huts of the Chinese laborers — the division hands of the railroad. They would step aside from the track and give us a mere passing look, returning to the track instantly, shovel in hand, giving the retreating train not a glance. So far as our observation went, they were models of industry and faithfulness. By their appearance and a peep into their abodes, we judged scarcity of water in that desert was not a serious drawback to these celestials. If cleanliness is a part of godliness, then "John Chinaman" is certainly a godless fellow.

Late in the morning we arrived at Elko, the most important town in Nevada, and the most prominent station on the Central Pacific, east of Sacramento.

Its importance arises from the fact of its being the center of the White Pine trade and travel.

Here we had an excellent breakfast at the Cosmopolitan Hotel, well kept by Mr. Treat. Many of us met old friends at this station, and spent a most agreeable hour in chatting with them and walking about the town.

INDIANS.

Moving on we soon reach Carlin, a place of importance to the road. Here we first met with Indians in any considerable number. They sat upon the ground near the station. In one circle eight or ten of the males were gambling for money. Near by sat an equal number of squaws, gambling for beads and bears' bones, their children playing about them. We were told that they belonged to the tribe of Shoshones. A more stolid, degraded, filthy, thievish-looking set of vagabonds in human form we had never seen. From others which we saw at different places along the line of the railroads, we had fears that we should never have our eyes gladdened with any specimen of the "noble red man" pictured to us by Fenimore Cooper and hundreds of his imitators since. From all that we saw and heard, the noble red man is "played out," and a mere remnant is left, half brute, half savage, lingering in a greatly modified human form.

HUMBOLDT CAÑON.

Soon after leaving Carlin, we enter Humboldt cañon, twelve miles in length. The Humboldt river cuts its way through this defile of rocks, running rapidly and angrily along its pent-up sides. This cañon, though not so grand as some we had passed, still was a scene long to be remembered. In the fantastically piled up rocks, without much imagination, we saw castles, bowers, vast fortifications, immense breastworks of contending armies, fallen temples, and abandoned, crumbling cities. The party, in that half-hour "run" through "twelve-mile cañon," lived months in feast of eyes and emotion of heart.

Here many thrilling incidents have occurred during the "emigrant times." Near this cañon a party from Arkansas were surprised by hostile Indians, while resting at noon, and instantly killed, with the exception of one of their number, who snatched up his rifle and retreated to the nearest cover, and there battled with all the energy of despair, killing several of the savages before being dispatched by the arrows of his assailants.

At Battle Mountain station we dined with the oldest hotel keeper of Nevada, Mr. N. H. Gardner. Before approaching the station, bills of fare were scattered through the cars. As we read over this metropolitan bill of varied luscious dishes, we thought, what would the emigrants, toiling and starving over this region, only a few years ago, have said, if assured that immediately on their heels the iron horse would draw up a train of passengers to a first-class eating station, within sight of the very spot of their deadly encounter with the savages? But so it is with this Yankee nation—"you can't most always tell, sometimes, when you least expect it the most."

From here on to Humboldt station, we pass over a country of not much interest except in its past history of Indians and emigrants, mines and hot springs. No vegetation meets the eye but the sage brush—alkali beds are frequent and the impalpable dust stirred up by the rushing train penetrates through the double windows of our cars, and produces some sore throats and lips.

APPROACHING THE SIERRAS.

At a late hour in the evening we supped at Humboldt, and push on in high spirits, knowing that in the morning our eyes are to be gladdened with the sight of the Sierra Nevadas.

We gather in our usual groups, and talk over the days incidents, the coming scenes of mountain and plains, and our advent into the metropolis of the Pacific on the morrow. We can never be grateful enough to that party of ladies, who made even the alkaline plains a sort of oasis, by their smiles, good cheer and uniform vivacity of spirits. Those evenings across the continent can never be forgotten. We watched this forced female society upon two veteran old bachelors — gradually we noticed their hardness begin to soften, the rigidity of face give away, and reticence breaking into a kind of chattiness. From the influence of that trip we are looking confidently in the list of marriages for the announcement that Mr. E. S. T. or Mr. A. J. M. were, etc., etc.

That night we retired to our beds oppressed with summer heat, somewhat restless and dusty. In the morning we awoke at Truckee with frosty windows, a crisp and bracing air about us. We had commenced the ascent of the Sierra range.

The ascent from Truckee mingles the grand with the beautiful. The first rays of the sun added brilliancy to the landscape and tinged the mountain peaks with gold. All were pointing out objects of beauty and grandeur. As we rounded a mountain peak, or pursued our course through a gorge, or darted through a tunnel, on every side, and ever, scenes awing, grand and beautiful, passed before us. The weight of the rails, and the solidity of the track, and the ease with which the locomotive moved our heavy train in this wild region of mountain cañons and peaks, drew forth unstinted praise from our practical party of railroad judges.

We mounted the engine and rode along this track among the clouds — now moving along on sideling rocks — now upon the edge of dizzy precipices, looking down a thousand feet upon patches of grass and silver streams. "Ah, but," said the engineer, "you ought to see it snow here — coming down in flakes as big as a pancake — to a depth of feet in an hour." We suggested that it was not really natural snowing, but that the clouds drifting along these mountains were punctured by their peaks, and their contents abnormally emptied. He expressed himself gratified with this new explanation of the heavy snowing of these mountain regions, only, he said, the less abnormal snowing the better for him and all concerned in railroading on the Sierras.

THE SUMMIT.

The summit was reached at an early hour, where we were met by Mr. S. P. Holden, Mr. Roe, Mr. Patten of the Cosmopolitan, and Mr. Ridgeway of the Grand Hotel, San Francisco. At the "Summit House," a most excellent breakfast was provided; all were in capital eating order, and did the good things provided ample justice.

After breakfast the party, guided by Mr. Goodman, who, since his meeting the party at Ogden, had been most indefatigable in his efforts to make us all perfectly comfortable, proceeded through the long tunnel on the summit (1,659 feet) to the mountain tops overlooking Donner lake. Here the party were for a moment lost in silent admiration of the beautiful landscape reposing in serene beauty far beneath them. However awe-inspiring the scene and sublime the spectacle of so large a number of persons thus quietly doing homage to the great Creator, it could not long continue. The pent up feelings of the party must have vent, and so with one accord they sang —

"Praise God from whom all blessings flow."

The party then scattered among the rocks in search of lichens, mosses and ferns, of which each lady brought away large selections.

A stay of two hours was allowed us at the summit, during which time we enjoyed ourselves as children, rambling over the mountains.

As we were on the point of departure, an agreeable surprise was given to us by our hostess, who presented four of the party, viz., C. W. Smith and lady, A. Hull and wife, Mrs. Evarts and Mr. G. L. Grant, with handsome cakes, neatly ornamented with sugar ornaments, and having the name of each fortunate recipient put on with the same sweet material. Much satisfaction was shown by the entire party for this marked kindness, and no jealousy was shown by those who were not recipients from the hostess. All understood the names were selected at random.

Refreshed and delighted by their stay at the summit, the party again set out on their journey westward.

After getting clear of the almost interminable snow-sheds, the grand scenery around us was greatly enjoyed.

A little above the forks of the American river, the observation car was attached to the train. In this the ladies, and as many gentlemen as could get comfortably inside of it, took up their places of observation. On went the train, at first at good speed, but latterly slower and slower, until it stopped on the brink of a precipice; and, as the magnificent view of the forks of the American river burst upon our delighted gaze, expressions of admiration broke forth from all.

After halting sufficiently long to give every person present an opportunity of feasting their eyes upon the grand mountain scenery, the train again moved rapidly on. Fifteen miles more of the same enchanting scenery, in which the long ridges of the Sierras, bristling with pine trees like huge *cheveaux-de-frise* filled up the back ground, we arrived, after several false alarms, at the real Cape Horn — a scene of sublime grandeur, unequaled on the whole transcontinental railroad."

CAPE HORN.

It is difficult to describe in words the sublimity of this scene. Our first sensation upon its bursting into full view was that of faintness, not from fear, but from intense awe. Here our train rested upon the side of a mountain away up near its summit, like a statue in a niche high up on some old tower. Down, down the precipitous sides of our mountain, 2,500 feet below us, we saw a silver stream — plats of grass — great trees that looked like garden shrubbery. Across a brief valley and mountain sides intervened, and on and beyond them peaks on peaks piled themselves to the skies.

Lengthen out that valley, raise those mountains but a little, and you look down on Yosemite from the track of the Central Pacific. We gazed long and enchanted on that scene of sublimity and beauty, and entered our train, saying, audibly, "Oh! Lord, how manifold are thy works, in wisdom hast thou made them all."

We move on, surrounded on every side by scenes of grandeur; descending rapidly the Sierra range, we pass through mining towns, looking upon hundreds of acres of "surface diggings" where man has toiled and sweat for the shining ore; we see miles and miles of "sluice ways" running parallel with us, over us and under us, across gorges and through mountains sides and all for gold. Now we begin to catch glimpses of the plains of the Pacific. We are rapidly descending into the valley of the Sacramento. With what interest did we look out upon this land of the extreme west. We should soon gaze upon the waters of the Pacific and walk the streets of its metropolis.

SACRAMENTO.

Sacramento is reached at 5 P. M. Here we stop an hour and look about the capital of the Golden State. Mr. Towne, General Superintendent, and Mr. Corning, Assistant General Superintendent, of the Central Pacific had joined us in the morning, and added much to our enjoyments by their attentions and care for us. And here we would remember with gratitude, Messrs. Kohler and Floring, and Messrs. Eberhart and Lachman, for sending refreshments for the use of the party.

On leaving Sacramento we were happy to find on board E. C. Fellows, Superintendent of the Western division of the C. P. R. R. We had rode many hundred miles in former years under his conductorship on the New York Central Railroad. The passage from this city to San Francisco Bay was through a beautiful and fertile plain, dotted here and there with an oak, which in the distance greatly resembled vigorous orchards. This ride of one hundred and thirty-six miles, under the guidance of Mr. Fellows, showed conclusively that "tall running" could be made on the Pacific roads as well as those of the Atlantic.

At Oakland many of the party were met by old friends, residents of California. Passing on to the ferry boat, the lights of San Francisco, five miles across the bay, presented a beautiful sight; the city being built on a side hill, giving at one view the gas-lights of numerous streets.

SAN FRANCISCO.

On the wharf at San Francisco we were met by carriages which conveyed us to the various hotels where we had been previously assigned. At these abodes of comfort and luxury we were at once at home; though our trip had been so comfortable, so well arranged, so leisurely made, that no one felt the sense of weariness. The writer, with some forty or fifty of the party, were located at the "Grand Hotel." We can say, heartily, this hotel well deserves its title. In its appointments we believe it is not excelled by any in our country. The especial attentions shown us by Mr. Ridgeway, one of the proprietors, was appreciated. Those of our party located at the "Cosmopolitan" and "Occidental" report genial hosts and luxurious accommodations.

On Monday, according to a notice issued by Mr. T. H. Goodman, the party met at 11 A. M., in the museum of the Mercantile Library, to form a permanent organization for the purpose of carrying out most effectually the different visits and excursions to be made. After a handsome welcome by Mr. Goodman to the Pacific coast, W. W. Chandler was called to the chair, and in due form appointed Messrs. Weed, Rhodes and Cannon a "committee" to nominate permanent officers. They reported C. E. Follett for presdent, and Sam'l Powell for secretary.

Hereupon Mr. Goodman read numerous invitations to the party: From the proprietors of Woodward's Garden; a general invitation from the managers of the California Theatre; an invitation from the Superintendent of the San Jose Railroad to pass over the road through the Santa Clara valley to San Jose; from Mr. Ralston, to accept his hospitality at his private residence at Belmont, on our return from San Jose; an invitation from the officers of the Agricultural Park.

A hearty vote of thanks for all these invitations was tendered by the party.

A committee was appointed to procure a suitable badge for each of the party.

The chairman appointed the following gentlemen as a standing committee: J. F. Aglar, L. Carvell, F. N. Myers, A. A. Folsom and L. P. Grant.

It was announced that the managers of the Mercantile Library extended the freedom of the entire institution to the party during their stay in the city.

SIGHT SEEING.

After adjournment, all of the party, eager to know something of the objects of interest in and around the city, scattered in every direction; some to the Cliff House, to look out on the Pacific, and to view that wonderful sight, the sea-lions working themselves up upon a ledge of rocks, a few rods from the shore, barking and sporting with each other, and then plunging into the deep. Others visited Woodward's Gardens, and were delighted with the sight of his wonderful eollection of animals, and with the beauty and variety of his trees and flowers.

Others, still, visited "Lone Mountain," the city of the dead. The vast area covered with graves showed that death had its numerous victims on the Pacific shore. Among the monuments most notable we noticed those of Senators Broderick and Baker—two men with a favorable national reputation—both dying tragically. At Mission Dolores (the original San Francisco) we saw the little chapel, with its tile roof and its rough walls, cracked and scarred by repeated earthquakes, but still serviceable. Around this quaint church is a cemetery filled to repletion with graves. Here are the graves of Corry and Casey, who died of hanging by the vigilance committee. On the tombstone of the former is engraved, "May God have mercy on my persecutors." It was remarked by our guide, an old citizen and one of that celebrated vigilance committee, "Poor Corry should have spared no prayers on others; he needed them all for himself."

On Tuesday our party met again, in the museum of the Library building, at 11 o'clock, and were called to order by Mr. Follett, the president. An invitation was read from the Mission and Pacific Woolen Mills, requesting a visit from the party to inspect their works, and to note the improvements made on this coast in the woolen trade; which was accepted.

Tickets for the Agricultural Park Fair were distributed among the excursionists.

NEILSON'S SPEECH.

Mr. Neilson was introduced by the president, and in a few remarks referred to the benefits that would accrue to the United States and the Australian colonies by the railroads, and also by the establishment of a subsidized steamship line between the two countries.

Mr. Neilson said, in substance: The Pacific railway has been ostensibly constructed to accommodate the traffic of some 700,000 persons, residents of the Pacific slope. But there were over 2,000,000 in the golden lands of Australia and New Zealand, as active, enterprising, wealthy, as fond of travel, as we are, to whom our great transcontinental railway is destined to become an accommodation fully as great as it is to us. These colonies have an immense passenger traffic with Great Britain. That traffic had hitherto passed along two routes: first, by steamers up the Red sea, thence by railroad across the isthmus of Suez, and then again by steamers up the Mediterranean. This voyage was accomplished in fifty-six days, at a cost of not less than $600 for a first class passage. Second class passengers are not taken along this line at all. The other route was by sailing vessels around the "Horn." The passage was a stormy, uncomfortable and tedious one, that averaged 100 days, and cost $400, first class.

The Red sea route, during three or four months of the year, was so exceedingly unhealthy as to deter all persons, not absolutely compelled by business, from traveling along it. For a moment let us consider what we have to offer as a substitute for these two routes. From England to New York we have the finest steamers in the world, averaging the trip in nine days. Then we have our grand transcontinental railway, with all the varied experiences it opens up to the traveler, accomplishing the space, from ocean to ocean, in less than seven days. Steamers averaging twelve knots per hour on the mild Pacific, and that, though much less than is now steamed on the more stormy Atlantic, would, nevertheless, reach Melbourne in twenty days. Thus, the whole voyage between

England and Australia would occupy but thirty-six days, or, if to allow for stoppages, say forty days, we still accomplish the distance in at least a fortnight less than by the unhealthy Red sea route.

He need not tell business men that such a saving of time, to say nothing of the other great advantages, would, of itself, settle the whole question as to which channel the trade would take. To show what that trade amounted to, he would mention that the imports and exports of Australasia equaled $75,000,000 per annum. Last year, $6,000,000 were paid for first class passages alone, between Australasia and Great Britain.

Much might be said of the ultimate advantages that would flow to this country from such a stream of wealth passing through it as would be induced to pass this way. His present purpose, however, was to show that a large railway traffic might be expected as the result of the establishment of a first class steam line from San Francisco to the colonies.

A bill was already before congress granting a subsidy to such a line, and would come up early next session. It was in the interest of the railway men to use their influence to secure the passage of that bill, as, without a subsidy, no steam line could compete with the wealthy Peninsula and Oriental Company, which was so largely subsidized by the English government, and took the mails and traffic *via* the Dead sea. Then it might be a matter for railway men to consider how far it would be wise to make special arrangements to encourage and open up this special traffic.

Mr. Neilson was listened to with intense interest in the portrayal of his feasible project. He was invited to address the railroad convention about to meet in Chicago. He there made a clear, convincing and exhaustive speech upon the same subject.

Mr. Goodman announced that Messrs. Eldridge and Irwin had tendered a steamer for the use of the excursionists Thursday. A letter was received from the N. P. T. Co., offering a steamer for Friday, but on account of the departure of the party on that day, it could not be accepted.

Col. Albert S. Evans and others offered to escort the various members of the party to the different parts of Chinatown, and the principal warehouses in the city.

An invitation was received from Messrs. Kohler & Frohling, and Messrs. Eberhart & Lachman, to visit their wine establishments.

CHINESE QUARTERS.

Immediately after the adjournment, the party formed into various small squads, and wandered off, some to the Pacific Mission Woolen Mills, while a larger party still, under the guidance of a few gentlemen of the city (who volunteered), proceeded down town, to pay a visit to the Chinese quarters, and to inspect the wholesale houses in that neighborhood. The first place visited was the house of Chy Lung & Co., on Sacramento street, where the party inspected the various fancy goods, silks, satins and articles of ornament, sold by this firm. After a thorough examination, the gentlemen proceeded up the street to the store of Tong, Chong & Co., 743 Sacramento street, where China teas and articles of household use are kept for sale. Here the Chinese money, denominated "cash," was freely distributed among them. Cups of tea were also passed round. At this place, Yee Teen, one of the firm of Yu Yuen & Co., opposite, invited all comprising the party to visit a Chinese restaurant, and, accepting his offer, the excursionists adjourned to the Hong Fa Low, on the west side of Dupont, between Sacramento and Commercial streets. Here the party partook of a lunch which was gotten up impromptu, consisting of various styles of cakes and teas, and also of cigars. Yee Teen, who is one of the proprietors of the restaurant, amused his guests with several airs, among which was "John Brown," on a three-stringed fiddle.

Thanking the proprietors for their kindness, and feeling a desire to see the mode and place of worship of these people, the party proceeded to the

" Ning Teong " temple, on Dupont alley, near Pacific street. A request to view the interior having been extended, all mounted the stairs, and, on the second floor, were greeted with a sight of some newly landed immigrants, who had not yet been assigned to work. Still up, on the third story, the visitors were fairly amazed at the sight which was presented. Curious carvings and castings, the image of " Joss " in satins and silks, the panoply and various dresses, curious inscriptions and other objects, were to be seen in all directions. The most attractive object, however, was the " Antique Bell," cast some 2,000 years since; which is rung during festival service, to keep off the evil spirits. From here the party went to the wine establishment of Messrs. Landsberger & Co., on Jackson street, where they were courteously received by Mr. L., and the various operations of bottling, corking, removing sediment, and all the various manipulations of champagne manufacture, explained.

TRIP DOWN THE COAST.

Wednesday morning, according to arrangements, we were to make an excursion on the San Jose railroad. At 12:30 o'clock, the party congregated on Market street, in front of the " Grand Hotel " where they were taken by the Market street cars to the San Jose depôt. Here four cars awaited us, and we started on our trip propitiously and pleasantly, T. H. Goodman still acting as master of ceremonies, as he had done since our arrival. We considered it fortunate that we had fallen into the hands of a gentleman so thoroughly competent, and so intimately acquainted with the characteristics of the coast. All felt the peculiar appropriateness of purchasing and presenting some token of our appreciation before, the breaking up the party to Messrs. Goodman and Keim. Accordingly, the matter was easily accomplished, under the suggestion and lead of Mr. St. John of the Chicago and Rock Island road.

We were all delightfully surprised by the evidences of agricultural wealth in the San Jose valley through which we were passing. Substantial farm houses and elegant country residences dotted the view on either side, and the evidence of refinement and luxury were visible everywhere.

SAN MATEO.

The first halt was at San Mateo, at the princely residence of Alvinza Hayward. The cars stopped within a few hundred yards of the house. Our course led us through a beautiful winding avenue, cleanly graveled, and bordered by flowers of the richest hue, and shrubbery of the most rare and beautiful varieties.

Then we were conducted to the stable, which is a palace of itself, being far more elegant in all of its appointments than the residence of many a wealthy man.

On one side of the gallery are single stalls, and on the other, double ones, or rather rooms, for each double stall is completely inclosed like a room, having a door, with a lock and key, and appearing more like a private apartment set aside for the use of a guest, than quarters for the equine pets of the princely proprietor. The stalls are littered with the cleanest straw, the rear of which is bordered by a rush matting extending the whole length of the range of stalls, and evidently placed there more for ornament than utility. No kitchen floor is more scrupulously clean than the floor of the main gallery between the ranges of stalls. The wooden divisions between the stalls are each surmounted by tasteful designs of iron-work. The whole visible wood-work, except the floor, is composed of alternate strips of red-wood and Oregon white pine, which are varnished, presenting a very rich and finished appearance. No paint is to be seen around the stable. Water is brought into the stable by pipes. Gas is supplied from the same source which supplies the house—a gasometer. A telegraphic instrument connects with the house, so that the proprietor may give orders to his hostlers without commanding their presence. Few of the guests had seen any thing to compare with this in elegance, and all were enthusiastic in praise of the consummate taste displayed. The hostlers brought out of her private apartment (one of the double palatial stalls referred to) the little beauty of a bay colt, "San Mateo Maid," of Hambletonian stock, three years old, which excited the admiration of the judges of horse-flesh, of which there were many along.

Leaving the main stable the visitors entered the carriage-room, which was well stocked, in accordance with other appointments. Opening from this to the right is the harness-room, carpeted and furnished with chairs and a sofa. The harness are kept in the most complete order, and are preserved from dust by a glass case with black walnut frame, which occupies two sides of the room. Up stairs is an immense hay-loft, with a capacity for several hundred tons of hay.

It was said that "Old Ben. Wade" was here not long since, and remarked, after looking over this extravagant horse-house, "Well, if I was not a man, I would like to be a horse in California."

Leaving the stable, we strolled around the grounds, the pleasure part of which occupy twelve acres. Surrounding them is a private race track, always in fine condition. The ample grounds are laid out with the most artistic skill. Water is supplied from a large reservoir, distant four miles in the mountains, and brought in for the special use of Mr. Hayward's princely mansion and grounds.

Every variety of vegetation that money will procure may here be seen. Evergreens of all descriptions, twenty or thirty varieties of the acacia, beautiful bunches of pampas grass, immense bay trees, and flowers and foliage of almost innumerable variety, combine to produce an effect akin to fairy-land. Indeed, it was more than once remarked by the visitors, during the course of the day, that the tale of the Arabian Nights was realized.

After a thorough tour of inspection of the grounds, the course of the visitors brought them, by the natural law of attraction, as it were, to the shade of a wide spreading bay tree, where were spread in tempting display a bountiful supply of the finest of fruits, huge bowls of iced punch, and the finest of wines, all of which received due attention from the thirsty and already somewhat fatigued guests.

FAIR OAKS, MERILO PARK AND BELMONT.

Again taking the cars, we proceed as far as Fair Oaks, where we found carriages awaiting us. In these the party took a rapid detour to the right, passing around and through the country seat of Mayor Thos. H. Selby. The limited time allowed gave us but a hasty glance at the fine orchard and beautiful surroundings.

On resuming the cars we were soon at the residence of Mr. Edward Harron, at Merilo park. Here we alighted and spent half an hour in rambling around the delightful grounds and through the large and sumptuously furnished house. The grounds of this residence are not excelled by any in point of attractive beauty. Their chief feature is their huge shade trees and velvety lawns, which more than atone for the lack of a large variety of flowers and shrubbery, as they are far more suggestive of retiring comfort.

Returning then toward the city, the party stopped at Belmont, the residence of Mr. Ralston, the cashier of the Bank of California. Carriages conveyed us to this elegant private residence. Here we spent two hours, walking through the spacious house, yard, stables, etc.

At about 6 P. M. 200 guests sat down to a most sumptuous dinner. Every delicacy and variety of food of that prolific country and clime found a place on those burdened tables.

After partaking of these regal hospitalities to the full, we were conveyed to the cars and set our faces cityward. Never had we spent a day of more unalloyed pleasure than the one we were now closing. All were in high spirits. A discovery had been made which was of some value to us, and that was, that the word "California" was a true shibboleth to test the articulation of a mouth that had sampled the native wines of the Pacific coast. We heard several, even of the more sedate of our generally exemplary party, attempt in vain the enunciation of that word.

In the evening the Chinese theater was visited by a portion of the party, many of them being ladies. They remained about an hour, after which they took a trip through Jackson and Pacific streets, viewing the delectable locality known as "Chinatown" or "Barbary Coast." They wended their way through these streets and adjoining alleys, laughing merrily at the strange and uncouth sights, and apparently in as high glee as when at the country seats of San Francisco's financial princes. They delighted in peering in at the windows, and with childish merriment would knock at the doors and windows of the close rooms, and laugh to see the astonishment of the inmates.

THE BAY AND THE GOLDEN GATE.

The next morning was the set time for the trip outside the Golden Gate, around the harbor, and the lunch on the P. M. S. Co.'s steamer *America*. Here we insert entire Mr. J. C. Furgeson's description of the trip, as given in the "Alta Californian."

"At nine o'clock the ladies and gentlemen of this party, with their friends, numbering in all about four hundred persons, embarked on board the splendid steamer *Chrysopolis*, which was tendered to the party by the California Steam Navigation Company. This handsome vessel, always kept in the best of trim, was particularly inviting. Gaily decked with flags, and got up expressly for the occasion, her appearance was such as would tempt even the most timid person to sail in her over our beautiful bay. Every thing on board was arranged so as to afford the greatest possible amount of comfort and pleasure to the excursionists. As those privileged to embark in her drew near to where she was moored, it was quite apparent that both her captain and crew were solicitous to receive their guests with all the warmth and free-heartedness of Californians.

"The officers of the California Steam Navigation Company, careful that their guests should enjoy themselves to the utmost, had secured the valuable services of the Second Artillery band, which was on board before the guests arrived. A liberal supply of choice refreshments had also been provided.

"THE WEATHER WAS PROPITIOUS,

And the arrangements complete; and so, amid the stirring strains of music and the heartfelt welcomes of the ship's officers, the party was received on board. Shortly after nine o'clock the *Chrysopolis* steamed from her moorings, and bore gracefully away across the placid waters of the bay. The band struck up and the merry dance began; refreshments of every kind were freely circulated around, and happiness beamed on every countenance. Many of our most prominent citizens had come on board to add to the pleasure of the party, and courtesies and congratulations were the order of the day.

"The *Chrysopolis* drew gracefully along-side the landing at Alcatraz, where it was intended the party should go on shore and inspect the fortifications. The tide being rather low, this was not done, but some of the officers of the garrison came on board and joined the excursion party. As the *Chrysopolis* steamed away from the island, the guns of the fort fired a salute, as if to add *their* deep voiced welcome to the many given to the excursionists before.

" After leaving Alcatraz island the steamer steamed down the bay past Fort Point,

THROUGH THE GOLDEN GATE,

And out a short distance on the Pacific. Going down, the fort, bristling with guns, and the rocky headlands of the southern peninsula, were much admired. The smooth waters of the broad Pacific especially pleased the excurtionists, each one of whom seemed glad to be able to say that they had sailed on its placid bosom. Mount Tamalpais and the light-house were both subjects of remark; and the beautifully situated town of Sancelito was pronounced 'real cunning.' San Quinten and San Rafael also received encomiums. Having sailed up the Racoon straits and round the Two Brothers, the *Chrysopolis* headed back toward the city, passing to the west of Goat island along the city front in full view of the shipping. Continuing this course, she sailed up Mission bay to a point from which a view of the Pacific rolling mills and dry docks could be obtained, when she turned back, and landed her much delighted passengers at the Folsom street wharf. Here they were conducted on board the

PACIFIC MAIL STEAMSHIP COMPANY'S MAGNIFICENT STEAMER 'AMERICA.'

Captain Warsaw, and the officers of the company received them on board, and led them through her splendid cabin. The interior fittings of the *Chrysopolis* had been considered elegant, but those of the *America* were absolutely dazzling. A splendid collation had been prepared for the excursionists. On entering her grand saloon, the display of crystal, silver, fruit and other dainties seemed quite overwhelming. All admitted they had never seen so much magnificence before.

"After the ladies and gentlemen of the party had inspected the tables, the guests were invited to take their seats and partake of the good things provided for them.

"Although two hundred of the excursionists sat down to the first table, there was still a large number who could not be accommodated. The officers of the company had foreseen that this would be the case, and, in order that there might be no weariness felt by those who had to wait, had prepared amusements for them. On the upper deck a large awning had been stretched to keep the rays of the sun from those who might be inclined to join in dancing, and here the band was stationed. Quadrilles, waltzes, polkas, etc., were entered into with greatest zest, and it would have been hard to decide who enjoyed themselves most — those enjoying the dance, or those enjoying the dinner.

"In a short time, so complete were the arrangements on board, and so efficient the large staff of Chinese servants who attended at the table, a fresh table was set, and those who had been dancing changed places with those who had already partaken of the princely hospitality of their entertainers.

"Nothing could exceed the complete success which attended this effort of the officers of the Pacific Mail steamship to entertain our railroad friends from the east. One and all, they express the most enthusiastic gratitude for the honor done them, which they say was beyond their imagination; had they not experienced it they never could have realized it.

"The size, strength and superb finish of the *America* were all objects of admiration to our railroad friends from the east. With our great transcontinental railroad, and such steamers as the *America* and others of the same fleet, what a vast Oriental trade can be developed! All the wealth of India and China must necessarily pass to the great markets of the world by this route. Reduced through-rates on freight will cause a much greater traffic than any that has yet passed over this route. The same far-sighted policy will also largely increase our passenger trade. The steamers similar to the *America* plying between this port and Australia and New Zealand, all the Australian travel to England, and *vice versa*, can be diverted through this country. Happily, our railroad friends can see all this for themselves. They have come here and seen our wants and capabilities. They have made our acquaintance in our own homes, and are able to judge of our energy and enterprise."

LAST DAY.

FRIDAY MORNING, SEPTEMBER 23. We realized that this was our last day on the Pacific coast. Our stay here had been one of unalloyed pleasure. Nothing had occurred to mar for a moment the overflow of pleasurable emotions. So attentive to our every want, so given up to our comfort, had been the railroad, steamboat and newspaper officials, and so generous and unselfish the hospitality of the citizens of San Francisco, that our stay on the Pacific coast was one of, if not *the*, brightest spot in our lives. One of our number expressed the feeling which pervaded all hearts, when asked on that eventful morning, "How have you enjoyed yourself, so far?" He replied, "My cup is full to overflowing; and when a thing is perfect I have nothing to say."

RESOLUTIONS.

At 11 o'clock of that day the party met at the Mercantile Library. Mr. Follett, our president, in calling the meeting to order, reminded us, as this was our last meeting in San Francisco, care should be taken that nothing requiring our attention should be forgotten.

Mr. Lewis Carvel, in behalf of the committee on resolutions, reported the following, which were heartily adopted:

1. *Resolved*, That the thanks of the general passenger, ticket and freight agents and other railway officers of the United States and Canada, now upon a visit to San Francisco, be tendered to the general officers of the Union Pacific and Central Pacific Railways, at whose instance they were induced to make the trip to California, for the kind consideration and courteous attentions so uniformly extended to them during the entire journey.

2. *Resolved,* That the thanks of the whole party are specially due and are hereby tendered to T. H. Goodman, Esq., the general passenger agent of the Central Pacific Railway, to Beverly R. Keim, Esq., the assistant general passenger agent of the Union Pacific Railway, and to John Corning, Esq., the assistant general superintendent of the Central Pacific Railway, whose presence, considerate kindness and attention have rendered this instructive and important trip one of unalloyed pleasure.

3. *Resolved,* That the thanks of the general passenger and freight agents and other railway officers of the United States and Canada, now upon a visit to San Francisco, are hereby tendered:

To the officers of the Denver Pacific Railroad; to the officers of the Utah Central Railroad; the mayor and corporation of the city of Omaha; to the officers and agents of the California Steam Navigation Company; to the officers and agents of the Pacific Mail Steamship Company; to the general officers and employés of the Western Union Telegraph Company and to the Pacific and Atlantic Telegraph Company, for the free use of their lines; to the officers of the Mercantile Library, for the use of their museum, and the privilege of using the various departments of their institution; to the managers of the California Theater; to R. B. Woodward, Esq., the proprietor of Woodward's gardens; to the officers of the Mechanics' Institute; to the officers of the San Francisco and San Jose Railroad; to Messrs. W. C. Ralston and Alvinza Hayward; to the managers of the Agricultural Park; to the officers of the California Pacific Railroad; to the superintendent of the Mission and Pacific Woolen Mills; to the officers and agents of the North Pacific Transportation Company; to Messrs. Gamble and Evans, who escorted the party to the Chinese business houses; to the officers of the California Immigrant Union; and to the *Alta Californian* and the San Francisco press, as well as to the citizens of San Francisco generally, for the courtesies, hospitalities and attentions they have so liberally extended to this party.

4. *Resolved,* That we leave the metropolis of the Pacific coast with the most pleasant recollections, and with enlarged views of her wonderful growth and commerce.

5. *Resolved*, That we recognize the vast agricultural and mining resources of the Pacific slope, and trust that the dissemination of such information as we may be enabled to impart at our own distant homes may result advantageously to the people who have so heartily entertained us.

6. *Resolved*, That printed copies of these resolutions, signed by the president and secretary of this organization, be presented to each of the general officers of the Union and Central Pacific Railroads, and to each member of this party.

7. *Resolved*, That the press be furnished with a copy of the foregoing resolutions.

CHARLES E. FOLLETT,
President.

SAMUEL POWELL, *Secretary.*

DINNER BY THE PROPRIETORS OF THE GRAND HOTEL.

Messrs. Johnson & Co., proprietors of the Grand Hotel, desirous of showing those of the party residing at the "Grand" a parting courtesy, invited them to a sumptuous dinner at five o'clock in the evening.

About sixty persons, composed of the ladies and gentlemen of the party residing at the Grand Hotel, and their friends, sat down to a dinner got up especially for them in Messrs. Johnson & Co.'s splendid style. The table looked unusually brilliant and attractive. At regular intervals along its entire length a number of beautiful bouquets were placed in glasses. These floral gifts were kindly presented to the ladies of the party by their entertainers as souvenirs of their stay at the "Grand." A noticeable feature of the dinner was the large variety of California wines supplied for the use of the guests. There were nine different varieties, all of the best quality.

The dinner was a complete success. Many toasts were drank, and many good-natured responses made. "The Prosperity of California," "The Press of San Francisco," "Johnson & Company," and other toasts appropriate to the occasion, were drank with enthusiasm, and fittingly responded to by gentlemen present.

RETURN.

After this sumptuous repast the party were taken in carriages to the steamer which was to convey them to Oakland, the Brooklyn of San Francisco.

On this steamer we found our Pacific friends—those who had rendered our visit so pleasurable—assembled to bid us good-by. On landing at Oakland, there was a shaking of hands and mutual regrets expressed at the parting. Entering the cars many of us received from these generous friends lunch-baskets filled with the most palatable refreshments; to many of the ladies beautiful bouquets were given; and thus it was that we left the metropolis of the Pacific and its ever to be remembered hospitable citizens.

And now the "Silver Palace Train" moves on, and we commence again to ride "across the Continent."

Mr. Neilson, an attaché of the *Alta Californian*, gives the following account of the return trip as far as Humboldt.

"HUMBOLDT, September 24th. "The railroad excursion party arrived safely at Humboldt at six o'clock this evening. The almost exclusive topics of conversation hitherto have been: California, her resources, and the magnificent hospitalities of her people. The party admit that they had been led to expect much from all they had heard of the Golden State previously, but they confess that they had totally failed to realize all that they had witnessed. The ladies say, that the trip has been quite an event in their lives, and that it will long continue to be the subject of pleasant conversation and reminiscence around many a fireside in their dear old homes. With one accord they pray 'God bless California and Californians!'

"Leaving San Francisco at 7 P. M. on Friday, the party arrived at Sacramento at 12:30 this morning. At that early hour the Sacramento *Record* had been put to press, and the proprietors kindly supplied the party with one thousand copies of the number, containing all the news of the morning.

"AT ALTA AND DONNER LAKE.

"Alta Depot was reached at 9 o'clock in the morning. Here a substantial and welcome breakfast was provided, to which the party did ample justice.

"Donner Lake was reached at half-past 11. Here Mr. Goodman, with his usual kindness and courtesy, arranged that the train should stop for fifteen minutes, in order to give all an opportunity to alight and drink in one long inspiration from one of Nature's masterpieces: the grand, the sublime and the beautiful. When the superlatives of the English language were well-nigh exhausted in giving expression to the party's admiration of the scene, they all with one voice and with swelling words and full hearts gave vent to their feelings by singing 'America.' Never, perhaps, was that noble strain rendered in more impassioned tones. At its conclusion, a venerable member of the party, with head uncovered, exclaimed with evident feeling: 'That scene should be a voice of assurance to us all of the existence of the Supreme Being;' to which there was a response of a hearty and emotional '*Amen*.'

"PRESENTATION.

"Off again, and at six o'clock in the evening the party arrived at Humboldt, where an elegant dinner was provided. Before the guests had arisen from the table, Mr. Follett, the president of the party, called the company to order, and requested Messrs. T. H. Goodman and Beverly R. Keim, passenger agents of the Pacific roads, to step forward, when they would be addressed on behalf of the party by Mr. T. A. Weed.

"Mr. Weed said: 'Messrs. Goodman and Keim: Gentlemen, It gives me pleasure, on behalf of this greatly obligated party, to address you, the representatives of the two great railroad corporations which have afforded us this treat — one of the grandest excursions of the age. On returning us to the shores of the Missouri you will have conveyed us by locomotive and palace cars over 4,000 miles across the continent, over vast plains, through awful cañons, around the summits and through the bowels of grand old mountains, until at last we passed the Golden Gate where the Occident and the Orient blend. Our hearts are full, our ideas enlarged, our conceptions of our country's extent greatly increased. It is a grander and more beautiful land to us, for this your favor. Our loyalty is doubly assurred by this continental trip. We shall never be content to dwell hereafter in any "pent up Utica." We know now how to sympathize with our countryman, who, having traversed this land from ocean to ocean, and from the great gulf to the great lakes, visited England, and declined an evening walk with his host for fear of falling off in so contracted a country.

"'No country, without these vast plains and far rolling rivers, snow capped mountains, Golden Gate and Union and Central Pacific railways, will be big enough to hold us in the future.

"'Gentlemen, after all that we had read and heard of this collossal enterprise of laying the iron rail across such vast regions, and upon and around such frowning mountains, we confess our anticipations are exceeded. We are agreeably surprised at the completeness of your grades, at the perfection of your track, and the equipment of your road. In these latter respects you can favorably compare with our best eastern roads.

"'It will give us pleasure, on our return, to commend the road for safety and comfort to all transcontinental travelers.

"'And now, gentlemen, as a slight memento of our appreciation of your unwearied attentions, and your care for our comfort and pleasure, you will please receive these precious jewels—the spontaneous expression of the gratitude of the whole party.'

"The cheers of the ladies, as well as the gentlemen, of the party, followed the delivery of this address.

"The pin presented to Mr. T. H. Goodman has a very beautiful garnet in the center, and is surrounded with diamonds. The presentation to Mr. Beverly R. Keim, assistant general passenger agent of the Union Pacific, is a very beautiful diamond ring. The presents cost $700. Mr. Goodman seemed greatly taken by surprise, as the gifts were entirely unexpected. He said 'he felt that he had only done his duty, which was to entertain his friends then present; he was a better worker than a talker; he was glad that this excursion had given him an opportunity to renew many old acquaintances among his early railroad friends. The beautiful pin would ever be treasured as a memento of their kindness and good feeling.' Cheers, of course, followed this speech. Mr. Kiem said, 'he would always treasure the beautiful gift as a memento of the happy hours they had spent together; it would be esteemed as one of the most precious of his household goods. The trip, to him, had been a season of unbounded delight; he was sure it would continue so to the end. He thanked them for their kind expressions of good will.' [Cheers.]

"The party then again sang 'America' in right hearty style."

No one not present on this occasion at Humboldt could imagine the picturesqueness of that scene. The place, the station, standing isolated and alone in a vast, uninhabited region; lofty mountains, plains and deserts near and in the distance; the station-house crowded with intelligent men and women; the beautiful train in front; the dining room filled to repletion by the hungry tourists; a score of "celestials" with servers in hand; the presentation; the enthusiasm; the good cheer,—all conduced to make it one of the scenes to be remembered.

Too much credit cannot be given to Mrs. Meacham, of the Humboldt house, for the really perfect arrangements she had made.

The whole party were profuse in their praise of the really splendid entertainments they received at this oasis in the desert. Marvelous, indeed, is the transformation the industry of Mr. Meacham has worked at this place. Here the effects of irrigation on a sandy, sage-brush country can be seen. To look at the garden of Mr. Meacham, full of rank, luxuriant vegetables, and know that only a short time ago it was the home alone of the sage brush, we were led to believe that all of our western deserts could and would be brought to fruitfulness at no distant day; and that the lines of the Pacific roads would ere long present to the eye the fruits and grains of the tropical and temperate zones.

ARRIVAL AT OGDEN.

The night of leaving Humboldt and the succeeding day we passed again through the alkali region, causing some inconvenience to the ladies, into whose throats and nostrils the dust penetrated. We reached Odgen, the eastern terminus of the Central Pacific road, at 3 P. M. on Sunday. The Sabbath had been spent quietly and in a way befitting the day. Services were held in coaches, at which there was reading of the Scriptures and singing of hymns.

At Ogden we partook of the first regular meal in nineteen hours. Here Mr. Goodman resigned the party into the hands of Mr. Keim. It was a pleasure for us to know that, though out from under the pleasant reign of Mr Goodman, he and his amiable and intelligent wife were to be our companions the remainder of the journey eastward. Here our Salt Lake City friends left us, and we bade them a regretful good-by. Here, too, Mr. Carvell and Mr. McMillan, of New Brunswick, left us to visit Salt Lake City, they having failed to make connections so as to visit that city with the rest of the party. We parted with these gentlemen with reluctance, as they had made themselves, by their geniality and companionableness, very agreeable to us all.

AN AFFECTING INCIDENT.

Parting with these friends reminded us of an affecting incident which occurred on our way west. One of our party, the representative of a brief road of twenty-five miles in the east, here gave out. The road was longer than he had calculated on The separation between him and wife and child and home was widening hourly. And then, too, the mighty stretch yet to be traversed; there was no telling whether we should ever get back over this interminable, almost endless, road. Many of the company had their wives with them, and, thus supported, felt a kind of reckless glee behind locomotives headed for a week in one direction. To such our friend could not look for sympathy; he therefore clung to a benedict from St. Paul and the writer for consolation and advice. We assured him of the similarity of our situation with his; spoke affectingly of the dear ones we had left at home; but that, however trying to the heart, we were now going through on the mere force of the will. Our friend heard us attentively and reverently, but nevertheless bade us, with choking throat and damp eyes, an affectionate farewell, and took the first train east. Under the genial influence of our ladies, and the happy faces of their husbands, my friend and I soon rallied from the temporary somberness thrown over us by this touching and very home-suggestive incident.

OGDEN TO SIDNEY.

From Ogden, we soon enter the lower Weber cañon, enjoying, as if fresh and unseen before, this pass in the mountains, and the whole ascent and crossing of the Rocky Mountain range. How we sat and mused and drank in and feasted on the mountain scenery over which we were rapidly rolled. Nor did the Laramie plains lose any of their beauties and pleasing diversities by a second view — we saw all from a different stand-point, and new sublimities burst upon us at every turn. As we descended the mountains into Cheyenne, the view was grand and imposing; on one side "Alps o'er Alps" arose — on the other, stretching far away with indistinct boundaries, or merging into the horizon, was the great delta of the Platte, which, melting into the prairies, reaches unbroken to the shores of the Missouri.

> "And the heart swells, while the dilated sight
> Takes in the encircling vastness."

And now we are again, at night-fall, at Cheyenne. We rush to the telegraph office and assure our friends, in the far off east, of our safe and happy progress homeward. Here again our party is depleted. Our Denver Pacific friends part with us. Mr. Nye and wife, Mr. Ward and lady friend, bid us good-by. A pleasant remembrance of them will linger long in our hearts. From their joining us to the separation, they formed an integral part of our enjoyment.

The party are to supper at Sidney, one hundred and ten miles east; the track is straight, the grade descending; the country through which we pass said to be one of the best grazing sections in the world; stock thrive at all seasons of the year, without care, upon the "bunch" grass which covers the valleys, bluffs and low hills. This ride to Sidney that evening will not soon be forgotten. The train was whirled along at a rapid rate — the first hour making fifty-six miles, and should have accomplished the whole distance at the same rate, but for the heating of a journal. So firm and well bedded was the track, so substantial the rolling-stock, that we hardly realized the rapid rate we were moving, and felt more than the usual safety under such speed.

RAILROAD MATERIAL AND LANDS.

And here let us say that nothing surprised us more than the abundance of good stone for masonry, at short intervals, upon all points of these Pacific roads. Water is also found in abundance for railroad purposes throughout those portions of the Sierra Nevada, Wahsatch and Rocky mountains, through which the road penetrates; also, water is found at every few miles intervals in the basins, where it usually occurs in springs at the bases of the mountains, and in small streams descending from the higher peaks and ridges to the adjacent plains. A simple reference to the map of the Pacific railroad route will exhibit an important feature in this respect, in the fact that in its remarkably direct course, for its great length, from the Missouri west to the Pacific, it follows the ascending and descending valleys of permanent rivers and their tributaries for more than two-thirds of its entire length, and that water is abundant on all the intermediate spaces.

Thus, it will be seen further, that the means of irrigation is at hand, to a large extent, wherever the lands are suitable for it. And we believe that most of the sage plains *are* suitable, from the fact of the rich odor and resinous property of that plant, and from the exceedingly nutritous character of the grass occasionally scattered through it. It is now an established fact, that the Mormons produce some of their finest crops from reclaimed sage plains.

We see no reason, in view of these facts, why, in a few years, the lands of the Pacific railway company will not be sought with avidity by intelligent agriculturists. The fact that irrigation will be necessary is no discount on the value of those lands. It is fast coming to be understood that irrigation is the only safe way of insuring a steady yearly crop, and that every farm crop can be produced cheaper by its help than on lands where it is not thought necessary. A recent writer has truly said: "There are not many acres laid down to grass in New England, whether for hay or pasture, that would not have justified an outlay of $10 per acre to irrigate them simply for this year alone" (1870). So much for railroad material and farming.

INCIDENTS, ETC.

At Sidney we sat down to a good supper. Here we met with our first and only unpleasant occurrence. While one of our ladies was at supper, a straggling soldier stepped into the car and walked off with her satchel, containing valuables, worth some $3,000. The loss was not discovered until we were many miles on our way. The deep sympathy manifested by the whole party toward the loser showed to what extent the party had become bound up in each others' interests. The husband took the first train west, and recovered the satchel and contents intact, telegraphing the good news in the morning to our on-moving eastern train. This removed all clouds from our faces, and we resumed our usual cheerful state.

Among those of our party who, from Omaha to San Francisco and return, exerted themselves to contribute to our pleasure and comfort, was Mr. Henry Starring, general baggage agent of the west. He was fruitful in expedients to relieve the monotony of the plains or the later hours of the evening. He, together with Col. Moore, who presided in the baggage car, exhibited such care of our valuables, such patience with questions about "the baggage," that the ladies presented each of them with a handsome memorial gift of appreciation.

Mr. Brown, the superintendent of the palace cars, will be remembered for his gentlemanly demeanor and accommodating spirit. He was a decided favorite with the company.

But we cannot discriminate among so many from whom we received attentions and favors. The gratitude of the entire party is due to all the officials and subordinates of these railways, who contributed so much to the happiness of the company and toward making the excursion an unequaled success.

NEAR THE TERMINUS.

And now we are drawing near to the terminus, where the party are to break up and disperse over our broad land. As we near the shore of the Missouri we gather in groups, and recall the varied scenes and marked incidents of our happy excursion. We speak of visits to be made to each other in our far-separated homes — of the renewal and continuance of the pleasant acquaintances made in this prolonged trip of beauties and wonders. We do not, however, lose sight of the mighty prairie over which we are gliding, and which sweeps up to the city of our separation. It was grand and beautiful. Far-lengthened and wide-extended, a prairie is ever an object of surpassing interest and beauty.

> "Lo! they stretch
> In airy undulations, far away,
> As if an ocean in its gentlest swell
> Stood still, with all its rounded billows fixed
> And motionless forever. Motionless?
> No, they are all unchained again. The clouds
> Sweep over with their shadows, and beneath,
> The surface rolls and fluctuates to the eye;
> Dark hollows seem to glide along and chase
> The sunny ridges. * * *
> The great heavens seem to stoop down upon the scene of love;
> A nearer vault, and of tenderer hue
> Than that which bends above the eastern hills."

PACIFIC ROADS.

And now we have passed over the Pacific roads. We had comprehended something of the grandeur of this collossal enterprise of laying the iron track across 2,000 miles of plains and mountains. We had seen that the road was a fixed fact. Passing and repassing, we saw it firmly bedded, strongly culverted, bridged, splendidly equipped and efficiently worked. We had seen villages springing up on its lengthened sides, and cities laid out which will soon bear the name properly and justly. With its eastern railroad and its transpacific steam connections, we saw that, by an enlightened view and a liberal policy on the part of all concerned, the most sanguine expectations of far-seeing statesmen would be realized, viz.: of making the American continent the highway from Europe to Asia, and to the ports of the North and South Pacific.

All felt, as we coursed over this great railway, and saw its connection with the splendid transpacific steamers plying with Japan, China, and the far east, that the prophecies of Thomas H. Benton, uttered fifteen years ago in the United States Senate, in a plea for the Pacific road, were on the verge of fulfillment.

Said that patriotic statesman:

"The Pacific road will be made. To reach the golden California, to put the populations of the Atlantic, the Pacific, and the Mississippi valley into direct communication, to connect Europe and Asia through our America, and to own a road of our own to the East Indies; such is the grandeur of the enterprise, and the time has arrived to begin it. The country is open to settlement, and inviting it and receiving it. The world is in motion, following the track of the sun to its dip in the western ocean. Westward the torrents of emigration direct their course, and soon the country between Missouri and California is to show the most rapid expansion of the human race that the ages of man have ever beheld. It will all be settled up, and that with magical rapidity; settlements will promote the road — the road will aggrandize the settlements. Soon it will be a line of towns and villages, cities and farms. And rich will be the man that may own some quarter section on its track, or some squares in the cities which are to grow upon it.

* * * * * * * * * *

"Twenty-five centuries have fought for the commercial road to India — we have it as a peaceable possession. Shall we use it? or wear out our lives in strife over minor matters, while a glorious prize lies neglected before us? Vasco de Gama, in the discovery of the Cape of Good Hope, and the opening of a new route to India, independent of the Musulman power, eclipsed, in his day, the glory of Columbus, balked in the discovery of *his* well-divined route by the intervention of a new world. Let us vindicate the glory of Columbus by realizing his divine idea of *arriving in the east by going west.*"

SEPARATION.

On Tuesday, September 27, 2 P. M., we reach Omaha. We had journeyed to the Pacific and returned, without the slightest accident — without a marring circumstance. All are in as good spirits as on the day we left this hospitable city *en route* for the Pacific.

Nothing in the way of an excursion could have been more perfect in detail or as a whole. All felt that this trip would individually be repeated at an early day. We shall be disappointed if, in the coming season, there is not a great increase of tourists over this wonderful road, and through this wonderful country. Our people will not much longer, we believe, flood the old world to visit places and scenes that have been crowded and described *ad nauseum*, while their own land, in its vastness, its plains, its great mountain ranges and rivers sweeping over thousands of miles, have never met their eye.

Let every man and woman in the east, who desires to make *the* one trip of life, cross the continent to the Pacific coast.

Passing over the Missouri to Council Bluffs, we separate. Here we bid each other farewell — a regretful good-by to many of whom, we fear, we shall never see again. Taking the four railways that lead out of Council Bluffs, we arrive in Chicago the following day at 2 P. M., accomplishing the return from San Francisco in *four days and sixteen hours*— the quickest time on record. And the great railroad excursion of 1870 is ended

www.ingramcontent.com/pod-product-compliance
Lightning Source LLC
Chambersburg PA
CBHW021410090426
42742CB00009B/1081
9783744727181